New Parade 1

Senior Authors

Mario Herrera

Theresa Zanatta

Consulting Authors

Alma Flor Ada

Christine Ewy

Anna Uhl Chamot

Carolyn Kessler

Jim Cummins

J. Michael O'Malley

Writer

Christine Kay Williams

Longman

Contents

1 My Class

1. Look. Listen. Sing.

Good morning to you,
Good morning to you,
Good morning, dear teacher,
Good morning to you.

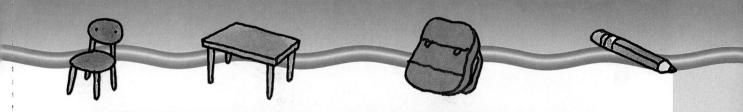

2. Play the game.

What's your name?

I'm Teresa.

3. Look and say.

red   green   blue

4. Look. Listen. Sing.

What color is it?
What color is it?
It's red. It's red.
The marker is red.

5. Read. Point. Say.

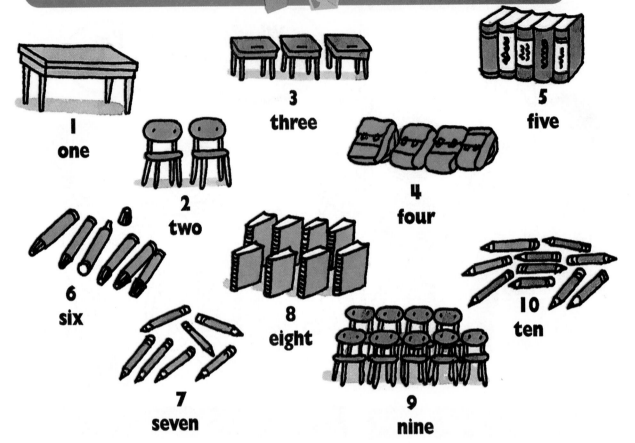

1 one

2 two

3 three

4 four

5 five

6 six

7 seven

8 eight

9 nine

10 ten

6. Listen and circle.

1. ② 4 6
   1 3 5

2. 3 7 9

3. 10 8 2

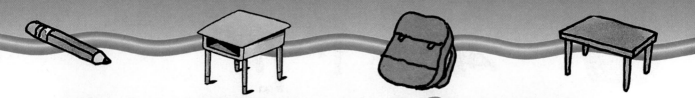

7. Draw and answer.

table

chair

desk

marker

What's this?

It's a book.

8. Look and color.

1 = 　　　　2 = 　　　　3 =

Ready for School!
by Mario Herrera

Good morning, Mother.
I'm getting ready for school.

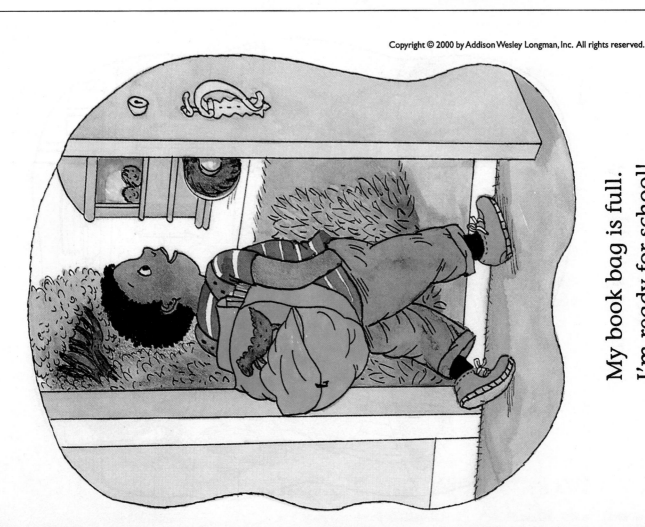

My book bag is full.
I'm ready for school!

Books to read.
Pencils and markers
to write and draw.

An apple, a banana,
a little red ball!

PROJECT

Draw. Color. Sort.

1.
2.
3.

Is this red?

Yes.

Count and say.

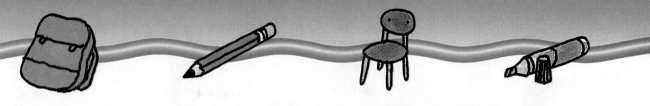

✓ Listen and circle. 🎧

1.

2.

3.

4.

5.

6.

✓ I can.

1. I can say colors.

Good-bye!

2. I can say numbers. **1 4 5**

3. What's your name?
   I'm _____.

2 My Family

1. Listen and chant.

My family has five people.

One, two, three, four, five.

We like to walk together,

One, two, three, four, five.

We like to sit together,

One, two, three, four, five.

We like to jump together,

One, two, three, four, five.

2. Listen. Count. Circle.

   1   2   ③   4   5

1.    1   2   3   4   5

2.   1   2   3   4   5

3.    1   2   3   4   5

4.   1   2   3   4   5

I'm David. This is my family.

This is my mother.

This is my father.

This is my sister.

This is my brother.

This is my baby brother.

Please tell me about your family.

4. Count. Say.

How many brothers do you have?

How many sisters do you have?

5. Listen and say.

Aa Bb Cc Dd Ee Ff Gg Hh Ii

Jj Kk Ll Mm Nn Oo Pp Qq Rr

Ss Tt Uu Vv Ww Xx Yy Zz

6. Listen. Write. Say.

A, B, _____, D, E, F, G,

H, I, J, K, L, M, _____, O, P,

Q, R, _____, T, U, V,

_____, X, Y, Z.

Mother, father, sister see

How I say my ABCs.

7. Listen and circle.

1. brothers 0 1 2 3 4 5 6 7 8 9 10

2. sisters 0 1 2 3 4 5 6 7 8 9 10

8. Count and name.

1.

2.

3.

9. Play and match.

It's a "D"!

They match!

10. Listen. Chant. Find.

A B CDE
This is my family.
F G HIJ
I love them every day.
K L MNO
Mother, father, baby, oh
P Q RST
Brother, sister, you can see
U V W X Y Z
All the people in my family.

Look!
Here's "B"!

I go to school and what do I see?
I see my classmates.
They read with me.

Then I go home and what do I see?
I see my family.
They are waiting for me!

I go to the playground and
what do I see?
I see my friends. They play with me.

I go to the zoo and what do I see?
I see monkeys.
They climb up a tree.

PROJECT

Make a poster.

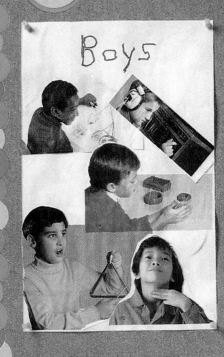 

Boys   Girls

Say the letters in order.

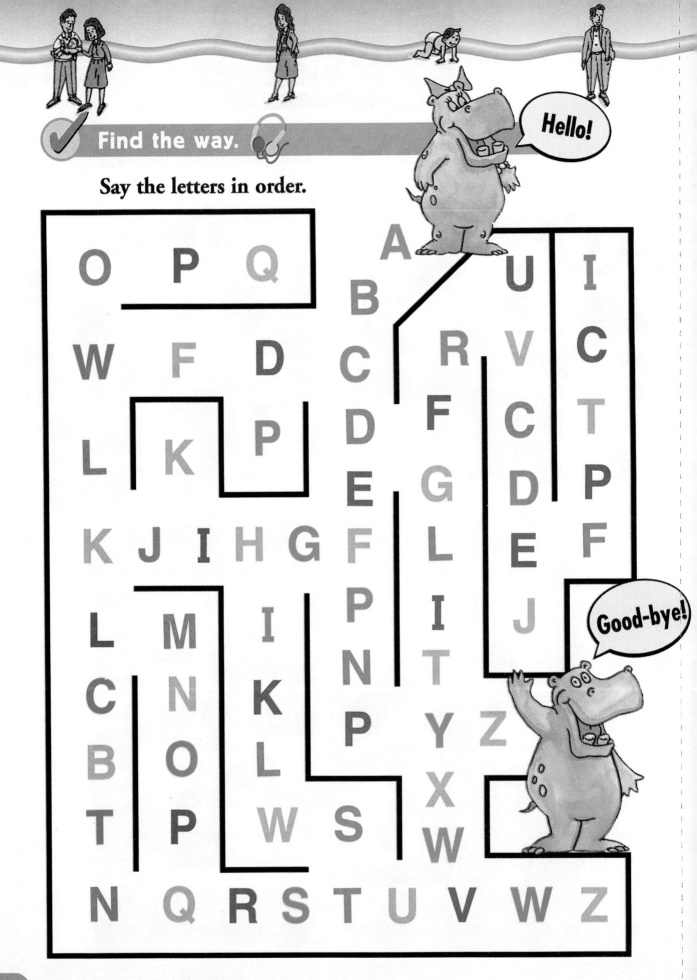

Hello!

Good-bye!

1. 0   1   2   3   4   5   6

2. 0   1   2   3   4   5   6

3. 0   1   2   3   4   5   6

4. 0   1   2   3   4   5   6

5. 0   1   2   3   4   5   6

6. 0   1   2   3   4   5   6

 I can.

1. I can say my ABC's.   **C D K T**

2. I can say mother, father, brother, sister, and baby.

3 My Body

1. Look. Listen. Say.

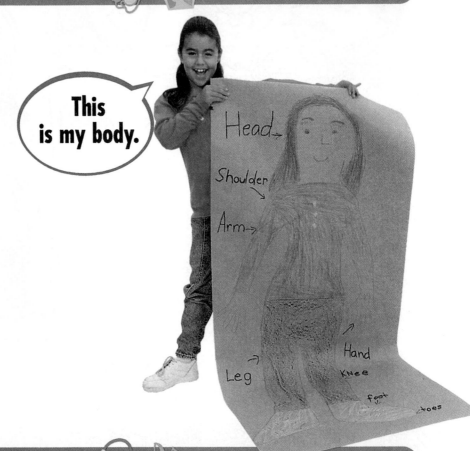

This is my body.

Head → Shoulder → Arm → Leg → Hand → Knee → foot → toes

2. Listen and sing.

Head and shoulders, knees and toes,
Knees and toes, knees and toes;
Head and shoulders, knees and toes,
Eyes, ears, mouth, and nose.

3. Look. Point. Say.

| yellow | brown | orange | purple |

4. Listen. Point. Say.

hair

eye

ear

nose

mouth

5. Look. Listen. Read.

What color are his ears?

They're yellow.

Look at this clown.
His mouth is big. It's orange.
His hair is short. It's blue.

Look at this clown.
Her mouth is little. It's red.
Her hair is long. It's purple.

6. Draw and say.

My hair is long and brown.

1.

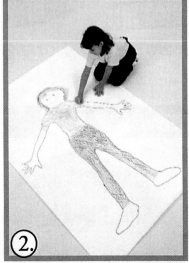
2.

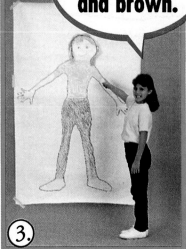
3.

7. Listen and color.

11. Play the game.

1   **2**   **3**   **4**

His nose is blue and his hair is green.

It's number 4.

12. Listen. Circle.

1.

2.

3.

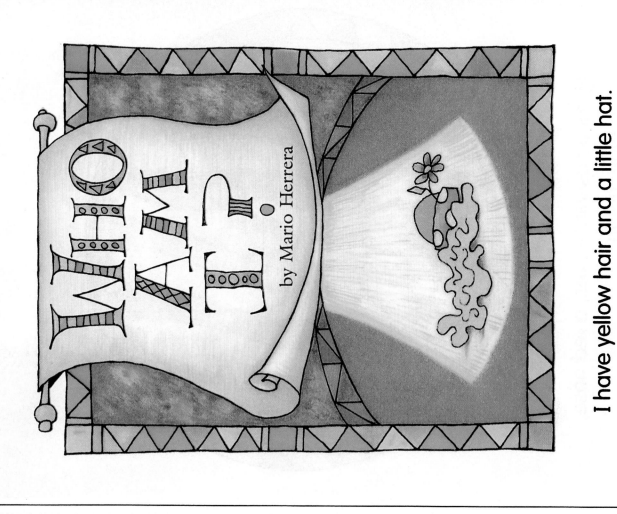

I have yellow hair and a little hat.

Who am I?
I'm a clown!

My face has white eyes, a red nose, and a blue mouth.

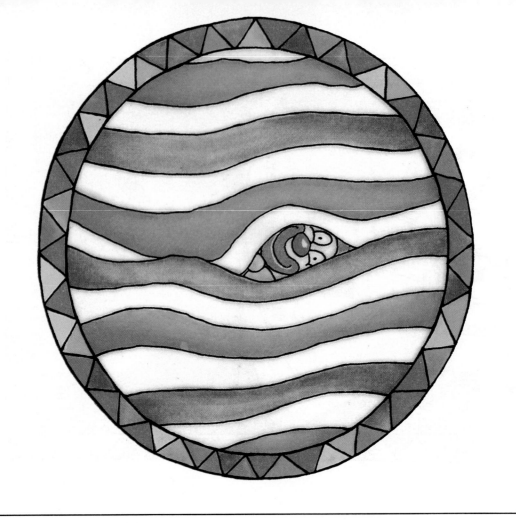

My clothes have many colors.
My shoes are big and brown!

PROJECT

Make a graph.

Is his hair short or long?

	1	2	3	4	5	6	7	8	9	10

Color. Make. Say.

It's Tony. His nose is orange. It's little.

Yes!

UNIT 3 • My Body • APPLICATION   **29**

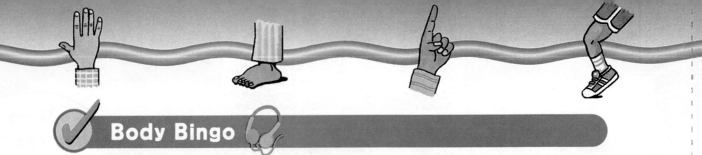

Body Bingo

Listen and color four more.

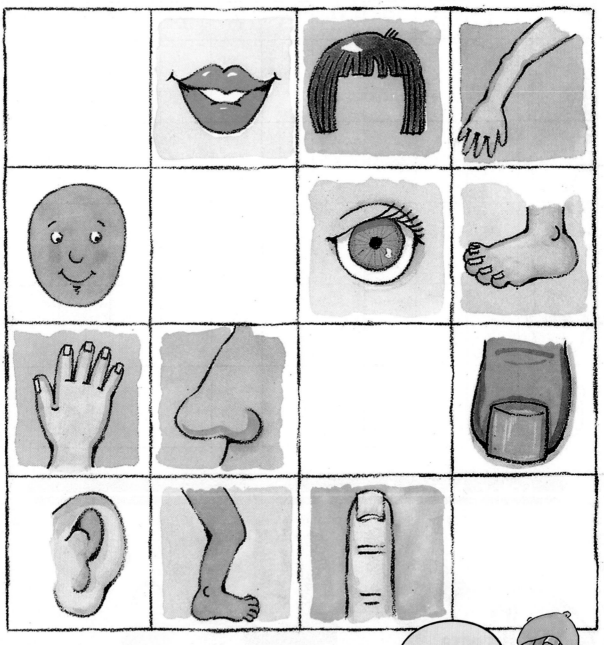

BINGO!

Listen and color.

 **I can.**

1. I can say eyes, ears, nose, and mouth.

2. I can say colors.

3. I can make a mask.

4 My Clothes

1. Listen and chant.

Are these blue pants?
No, they're not.
Are these green pants?
No, they're not.
What color are they?
Can you say?
They're orange!

2. Look and say.

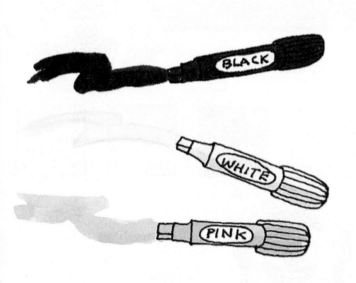

BLACK

WHITE

PINK

What colors do you know?

3. Listen. Point. Say.

dress

jacket

skirt

shirt

sock

dresses

jackets

skirts

shirts

socks

4. Look. Listen. Read.

I'm wearing a yellow hat.

I'm wearing black shoes.

What else are they wearing?

5. Look. Listen. Say.

What are you wearing?

A shirt and pants.

What are you wearing?

A sweater and a skirt.

6. Listen and circle.

  1.

2.  3.

4.  5.

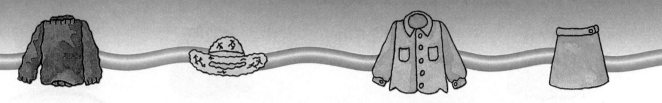

7. Listen and color.

8. Play the game.

9. Ask. Count. Color.

What's your favorite color?

	Favorite Color									
	1	2	3	4	5	6	7	8	9	10
blue										
brown										
green										
orange										
pink										
purple										
red										
white										
yellow										

What are your favorite clothes?

How many boys and girls like hats?

	Favorite Clothes									
	1	2	3	4	5	6	7	8	9	10
dresses										
hats										
jackets										
pants										
shirts										
shoes										
skirts										
socks										
sweater										

Helping

by Mario Herrera

Please help me.
Hang up these dresses.

1

Now you can put on your jackets.
Go out and play!

4

Fold these skirts and pants.
Hang up these shirts.

2

Put these shoes away.

3

PROJECT

Cut. Color. Play.

What's he wearing?

He's wearing blue pants.

Make a collage.

1.

2.

3.

These are my favorite clothes.

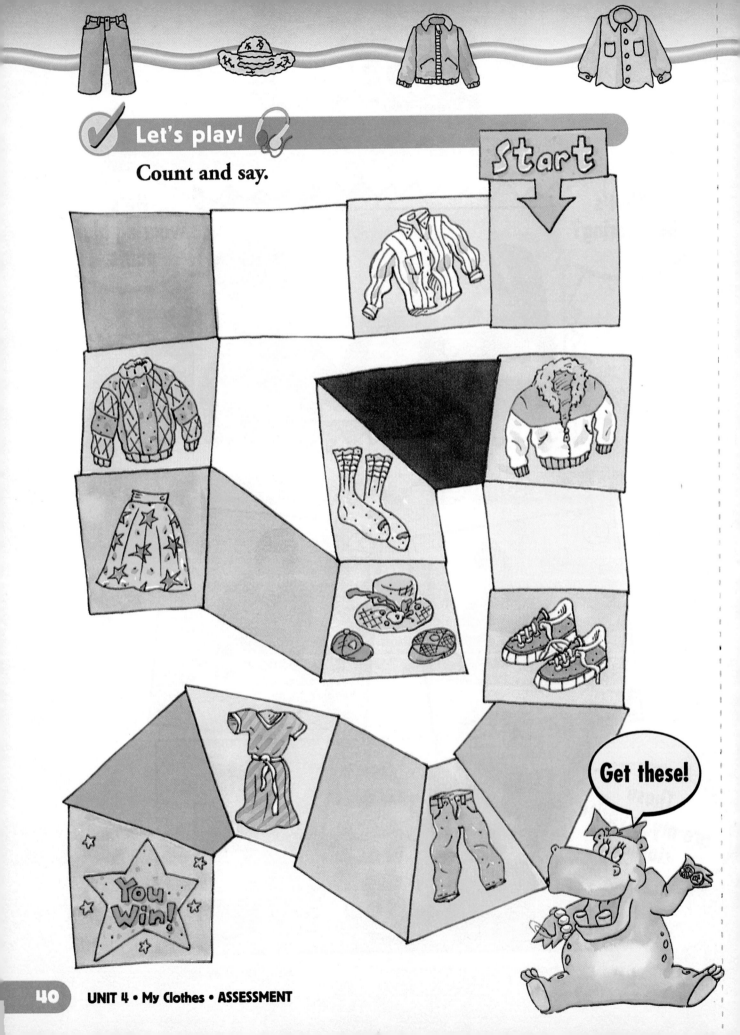

Let's play!

Count and say.

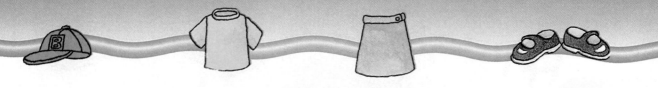

✓ Listen and circle. 🎧

1.

2.

3.

4.

5.

6.

✓ I can.

1. I can say colors.

2. I can say clothes.

1. Listen. Point. Say.

Hanna, where's the father?

bathroom

bedroom

closet

kitchen

dining room

living room

In the kitchen, I think.

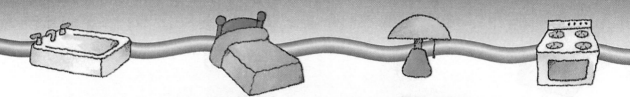

2. Listen. Repeat. Do the actions.

My House

Let's go to my house.
Let's go today.
I'll show you all the rooms
Where we work and play.

Here is the kitchen
Where Mother cooks for me.
Here is the living room
Where I watch TV.

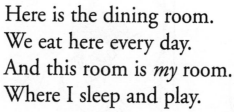

Here is the dining room.
We eat here every day.
And this room is *my* room.
Where I sleep and play.

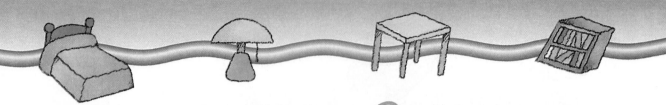

3. Listen. Draw your house.

This is my house.

4. Listen. Say the actions.

He's playing.

He's sleeping.

She's reading.

She's watching TV.

They're cooking.

5. Look. Match. Draw a line.

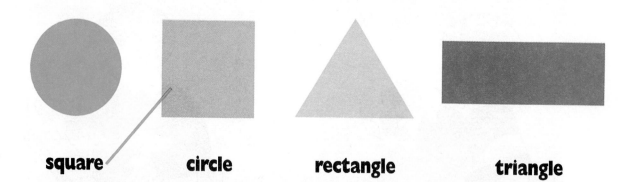

square   circle   rectangle   triangle

6. Count. Write the number.

How many red circles do you see?

1

1.____      2.____   3.____

4.____      5.____   6.____

7. Color. Cut. Listen and glue.

1.

2.

3.

Fluffy Is Missing!

by Mario Herrera

Mary is sad. Her cat Fluffy is missing.
Where is Fluffy? Where is Fluffy?

1

Fluffy is on the roof!
Now Mary is happy again!

4

Fluffy is not in the kitchen.
Mary's mother is in the kitchen.
Where is Fluffy? Where is Fluffy?

Fluffy is not in the living room.
Mary's father is in the living room.
Where is Fluffy? Where is Fluffy?

PROJECT

Make a house. Say.

How many triangles do you see?

1. 2. 3.

Listen. Act out. Say.

Who has a big circle?
I do! I do!
Who has an orange circle?
I do! I do!

Say other colors!

Say other shapes! Are they big or little?

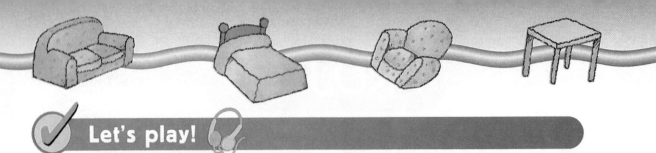

Let's play!

Say what it is.

	1	2	3	4
A				
B				
C				
D				

What's in A1?

It's a sofa.

Count. Write the number.

 _____1_____ dining room   1. _____ living room

2. _____ closets   3. _____ chairs

4. _____ beds   5. _____ bathroom

I can.

1. I can talk about my house.

2. I can name shapes.

6 Animals

1. Listen and sing together.

Meow Meow

Bow Wow

Neigh Neigh

Tweet Tweet

Moo Moo

Quack Quack

Ribbet Ribbet

Old MacDonald has a farm,
E-I-E-I-O.
And on this farm he has a dog,
E-I-E-I-O.
With a bow wow here
And a bow wow there,
Here a bow, there a wow
Everywhere a bow wow.
Old MacDonald has a farm,
E-I-E-I-O.

I'm a hippopotamus.

What are you?

2. Listen. Point. Say.

It's sleeping.

It's swimming.

It's running.

It's eating.

It's crawling.

It's jumping.

It's flying.

3. Count the legs. Say.

① ②

③

④

5. Listen. Circle.

1.

2.

3.

6. Listen and say together.

Do the motions.

Two little blackbirds

Sitting on a hill.

One named Jack

And one named Jill.

Fly away, Jack.

Fly away, Jill.

Come back, Jack.

Come back, Jill.

7. Look. Match. Draw a line.

Which animals are eating?

8. Listen and number.

1

CARNIVAL!

by Mario Herrera

The children are happy today. They are wearing animal suits for Carnival.

After Carnival the children are tired. Now they are all sleeping!

4

Frogs are jumping.
Dogs are running.
And big worms are crawling.

Little horses are eating.
Birds are flying.
And fish are swimming.

PROJECT

Make a book.

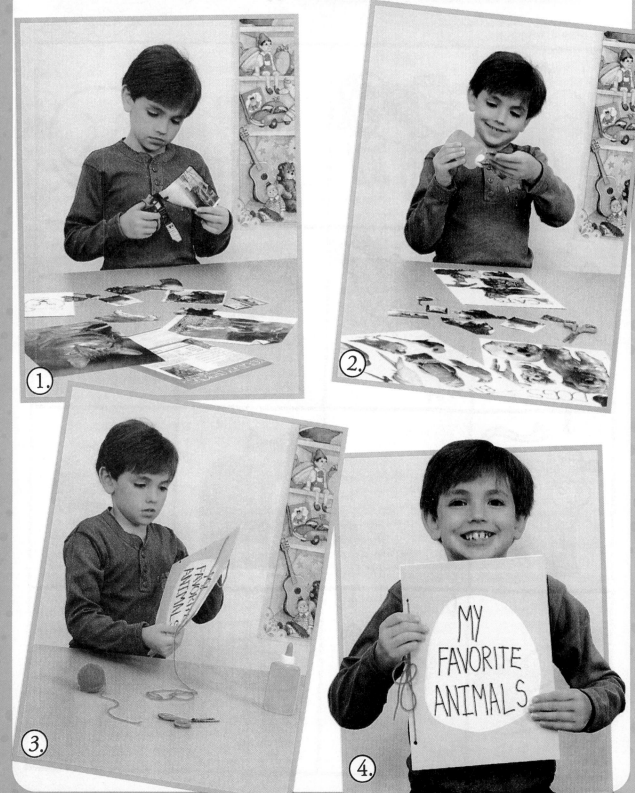

1.

2.

3.

4. MY FAVORITE ANIMALS

 Animal Bingo!

Bingo!

Listen and draw four more.

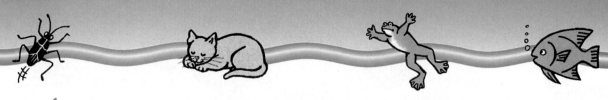

✔ Listen. Circle.

1.

2.

3.

4.

5.

6.

✔ I can.

1. I can say animal names.

2. I can say what the animals are doing.

7 My Birthday

1. Point. Listen. Sing together.

Happy Birthday to you!
Happy Birthday to you!
Happy Birthday, dear Carmen.
Happy Birthday to you!

2. Look. Listen. Say.

What day is your birthday?

It's Thursday.

3. Listen. Read. Say.

What do you have?

I have a kite.

What else do you have?

I have a big hat.

4. Point. Say. Number.

1 _____

_____  _____

_____  _____

5. Listen. Point. Answer.

What do you want?

I want ice cream, of course.

cake   milk

ice cream   hamburgers   hot dogs

pizza

6. Listen and circle the foods.

I want   .

1. I want  .

2. I want a   .

3. I want  .

4. I want a  .

7. Listen. Say. Do the actions.

What day is it today?

Monday, and Tuesday, and Wednesday,
Thursday, and Friday, too.
These are the days we go to school.
I think it's fun, don't you?

8. Listen and draw a line.

Sunday
Monday
Tuesday
Wednesday
Thursday
Friday
Saturday

9. Play the guessing game.

1.

2.

3.

4.

5.

6.

I have a hamburger, milk, and cake.

It's number 4.

Ana's Birthday Party

by Mario Herrera

Today is Saturday.
It's Ana's birthday.

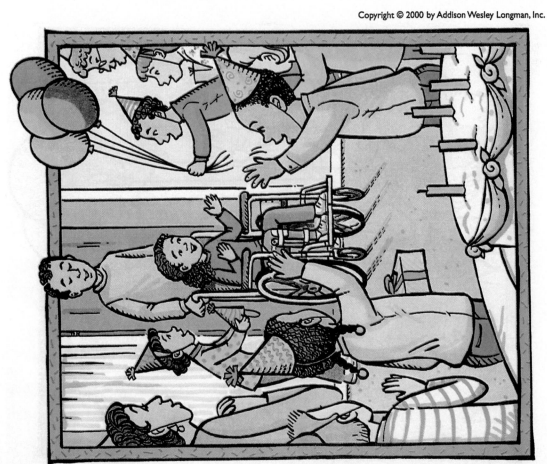

Surprise!
Happy Birthday, Ana!

The hats and balloons are ready.
The ice cream and cake are ready.

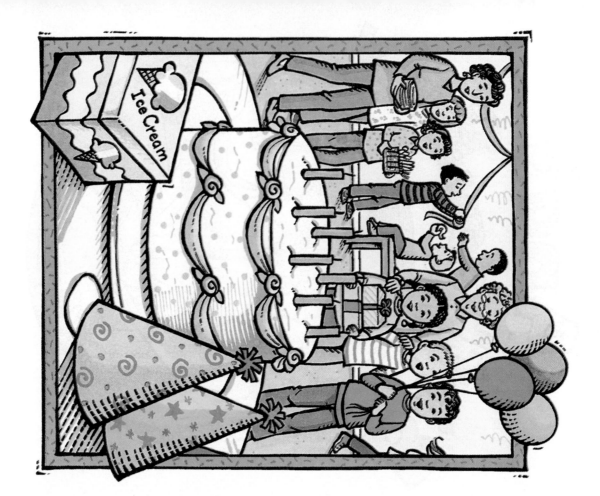

Ana's family and friends are here.
But where is Ana?

PROJECT

Play the fishing game.

Make the fish and say what you have.

1

2

What do you have?

I have a purple fish. It's number 9.

3

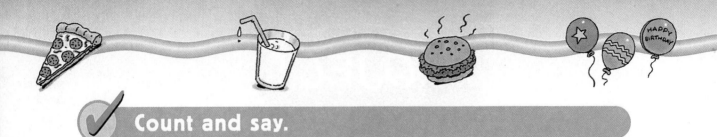

Count and say.

Tell what it is and how many.

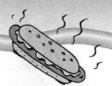

Listen and circle the foods.

1. I want a  .

2. I have  .

3. I want  .

4. I have a  .

5. I want  .

I can.

1. I can say foods.

2. I can say the days of the week.

SUNDAY	MONDAY	TUESDAY	WEDNESDAY	THURSDAY	FRIDAY	SATURDAY

8 My Toys

1. Listen. Point. Say.

What do you want?

I want the orange ball.

What do you want?

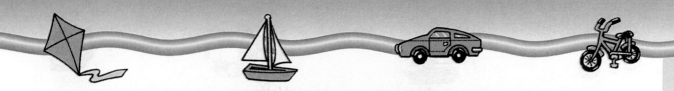

2. Listen. Say. Do the actions.

My toys are in my toy box.

I take them out to play.

And when I've finished playing,

I put them all away.

3. Listen. Point. Say.

Where is the kite?

It's in the box.

4. Listen. Point. Say.

11 eleven	**12** twelve	**13** thirteen	**14** fourteen	**15** fifteen
16 sixteen	**17** seventeen	**18** eighteen	**19** nineteen	**20** twenty

5. Listen. Read. Circle.

	13	(**15**)	**19**
1.	**16**	**20**	**11**
2.	**14**	**19**	**12**
3.	**18**	**17**	**20**

6. Listen and say together.

The Toy Store

I see balls and bats and cars.
I see boats and planes.
I see wagons, ropes, and dolls.
I see ships and trains.

I see games and tops and trucks.
I see bears and bikes.
I see swings and slides and skates.
I see drums and kites.

Of all the toys I can see,
I want one for me!

What do you want?

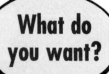

7. Look. Listen. Play store.

What do you want?

Here are the blue marbles.

I want the blue marbles, please.

Thank you.

8. Listen. Read. Circle.

The marbles are on the chair.
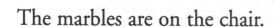

1. The dog is in the box.

2. The cars are under the chair.
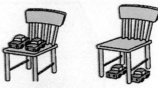

3. The ball is on the table.

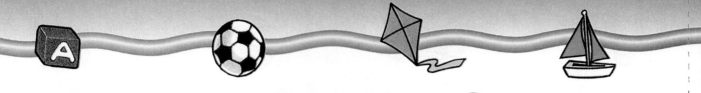

9. Play the Ruler Races game.

Count the squares and say.

10. Cut. Listen. Paste.

The Toy Shop

by Mario Herrera

There are many toys
in a toy shop.

How many toys
do you see?

Many! Many! Many!
We see many toys in the toy shop!

Fifteen! Fifteen! Fifteen!
I see fifteen blocks on the table!

Twenty! Twenty! Twenty!
I see twenty dolls on the shelf!

PROJECT

Play the Hide the Toy game.

Ask. Make a graph. Color.

Favorite Toys										
	1	2	3	4	5	6	7	8	9	10
ball										
bike										
boat										
doll										
kite										
plane										
skates										

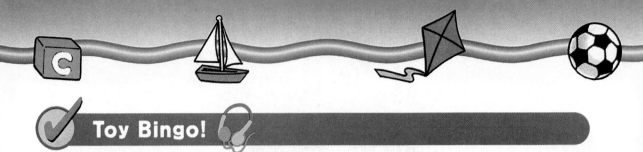

Toy Bingo!

Draw 4 toys. Then listen.

The red ball is under the chair.

Listen. Read. Circle. 🎧

1. The blocks are in the box.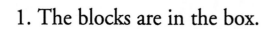

2. The marbles are under the chair.

3. The boat is on the table.

I can.

1. I can talk about toys.

2. I can say where things are.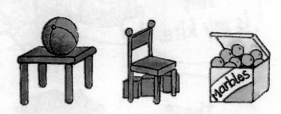

3. I can say numbers.

9 Having Fun!

1. Listen. Sing together.

If you're happy and you know it, clap your hands.
If you're happy and you know it, clap your hands.
If you're happy and you know it,
Then your face will surely show it.
If you're happy and you know it, clap your hands.

2. Let's show and tell.

This is my kite.

That's my jump rope.

These are my skates.

Those are my cars.

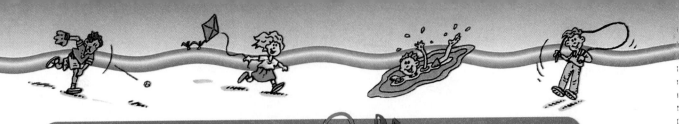

4. Listen. Sing together.

Is he skating?
Is he skating?
No, he's not.
No, he's not.
Is he riding his bike?
Is he riding his bike?
Yes, he is.
Yes, he is.

5. Listen. Circle the answer.

Yes, he is.
No, he's not.

1.

Yes, she is.
No, she's not.

2.

Yes, he is.
No, he's not.

3.

Yes, she is.
No, she's not.

8. Ask a friend. Write.

1. What's your name? _____

2. How old are you? _____

3. How many brothers do you have? _____

4. How many sisters do you have? _____

9. Listen and act out.

Playing Is Fun!

by Mario Herrera

Many children are
at the playground.
They're riding bikes.
They're jumping rope.

Many children are playing
at the playground.
They're all having fun!

4

They're kicking balls.
They're playing catch.

They're flying kites
in the sun.

PROJECT

Make a puppet.

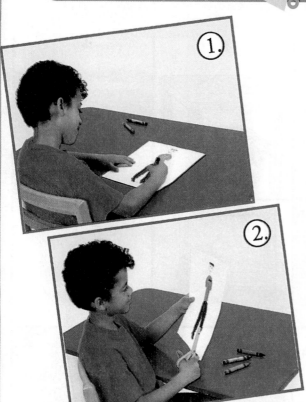

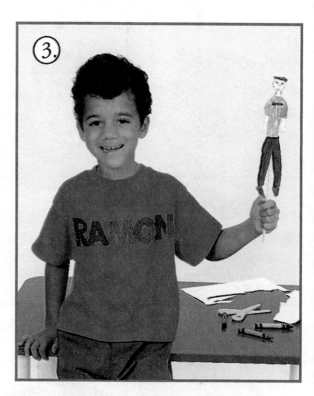

Make a puppet theater.

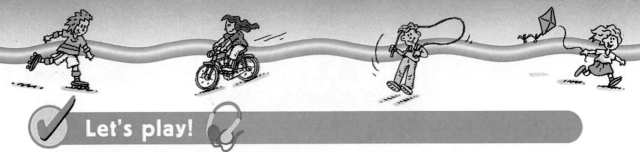

✓ Let's play! 🎧

Listen and find the picture.

Listen. Circle the answer.

1.

Yes, she is.
No, she's not.

2.

Yes, he is.
No, he's not.

3.

Yes, she is.
No, she's not.

4.

Yes, he is.
No, he's not.

I can.

1. I can say actions.

2. I can speak English.

2

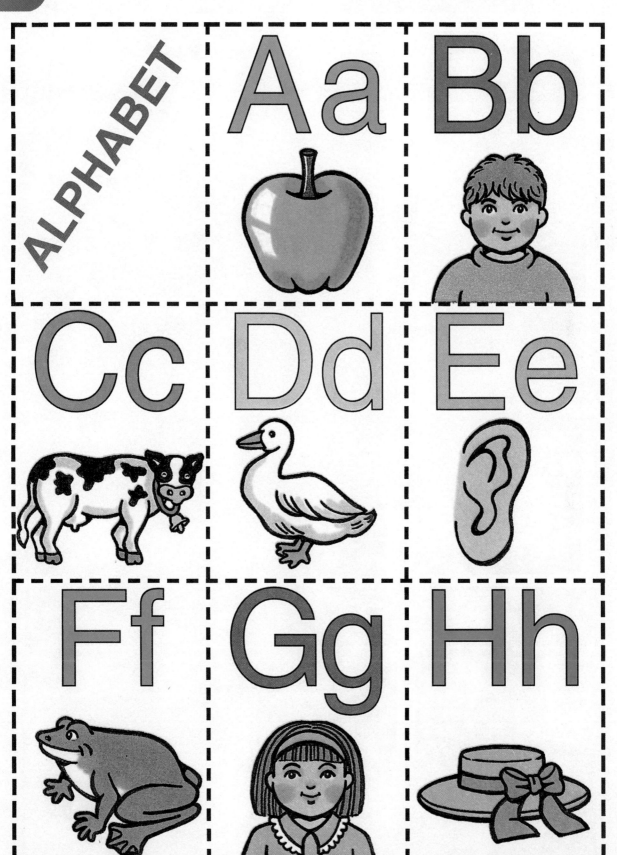

ALPHABET

Aa Bb Cc Dd Ee Ff Gg Hh

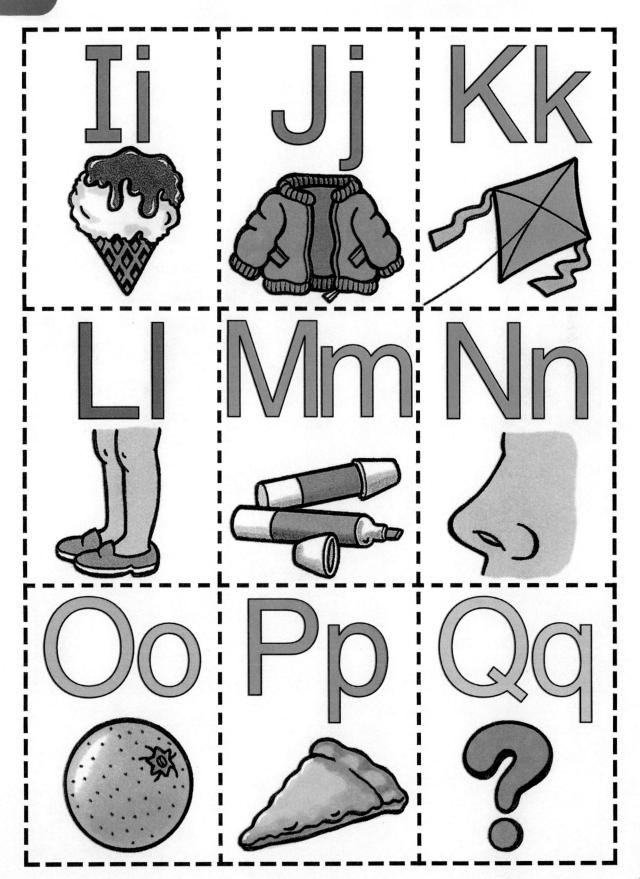

Ii Jj Kk

Ll Mm Nn

Oo Pp Qq

2

Rr Ss Tt

Uu Vv Ww

Xx Yy Zz

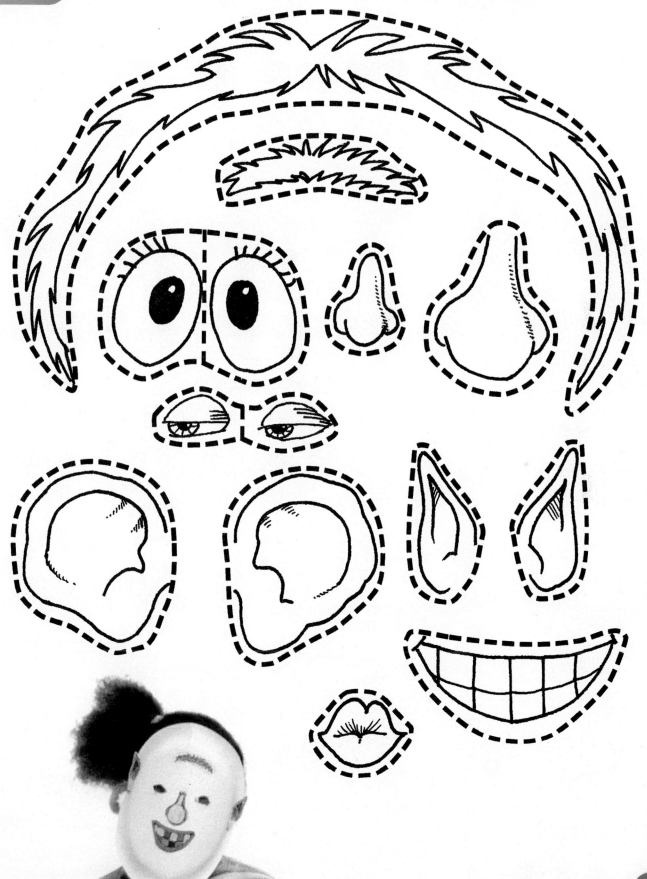

4

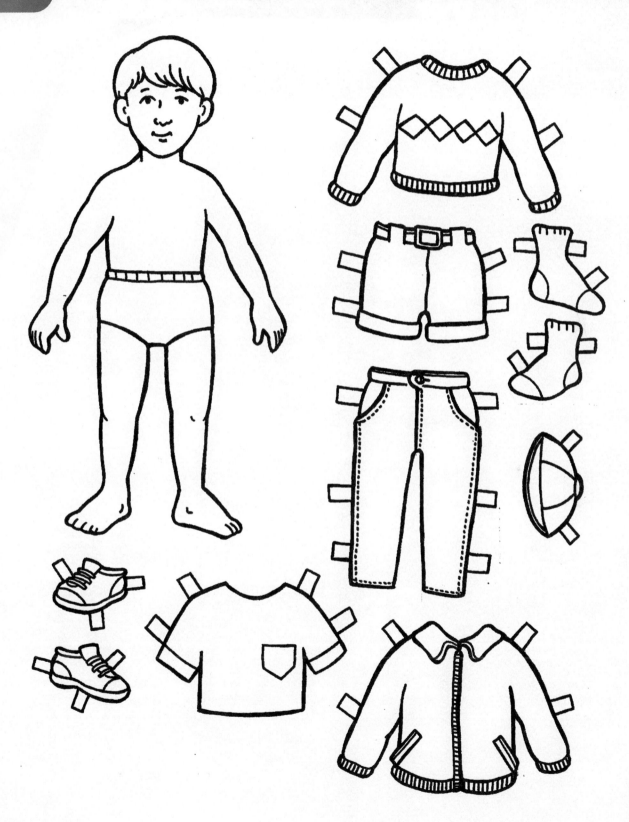

5

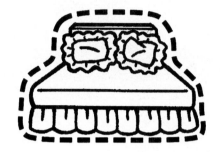

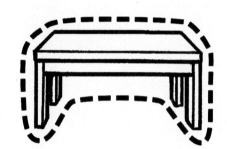

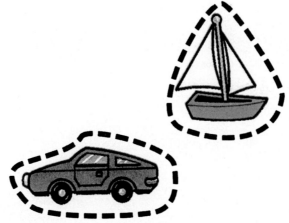

1
2
3
4
5
6